Can't I Just Start Over?

How to Own Your Mistakes, Make Things Right, and Move On

Written and Illustrated by
Jennifer Larsen

This book is a work of nonfiction intended to provide general guidance. It is not a substitute for professional advice. The author has made every effort to ensure the accuracy and completeness of the information contained herein, but assumes no responsibility for errors, omissions, or differing interpretations.

Originality Statement

This book is an original work written by the author and reflects their unique ideas, voice, and instructional approach. While it may reference common educational and career-planning concepts, all content, including structure, language, exercises, and framework, is the author's own creation. Any similarities to other published works are purely coincidental.

Printed in the United States of America

ISBN: 978-1-968756-72-7

First Edition

Cover design by Rachel Bostwick

Interior design and layout by Rachel Bostwick

For information or bulk orders, visit cantijust.com

A Quick Note for Adults

If you're flipping through this book before handing it off to a teen, thank you.

This isn't a punishment. It's a guide meant to offer some relief, some clarity, and a path forward for someone who may be quietly struggling. If they've made a mistake – or just feel like they've lost their way – this is a tool, not a lecture.

You'll find a full note for you at the end. For now, just know:

Your belief in them matters more than you realize.

Can't I Just Start Over?

How to Own Your Mistakes, Make Things Right, and Move On

Introduction:
You're Still You

Let's start here:

You are not a lost cause.

I don't care what you did, what you didn't do, or how many times you've tried and failed to get your act together. You don't need to be "fixed," and you don't need to reinvent yourself from scratch.

You're still *you*.

Even if things feel messy. Even if you feel like a walking disaster.

Even if part of you thinks, "Maybe I don't deserve to move on."

You don't need to burn your life down and rise like a phoenix from the ashes. That sounds dramatic, but it's exhausting – and honestly? You'd probably just end up smelling like smoke.

What you need is this:

To remember who you are *under* the problem.

The Issue Is Not All of You

Here's the truth nobody tells you when you're in a shame spiral:

Whatever you're going through – it's just a piece of the puzzle. One trait. One pattern. One moment.

It's not your whole personality.

It might be loud. It might be making a mess of your relationships or your future plans. It might have temporarily taken the wheel. But it's still *not all of you*.

You are not "bad."

You are not "too far gone."

You're not defined by the worst day you've had – or the thing you wish you could undo.

You're still made of everything else:

Your weird humor. Your quiet kindness. Your goals, even if they're buried under doubt. Your desire to be better. The part of you reading this *right now* because something inside still believes there's more ahead.

You Don't Need a Do-Over – Just a Shift

This book isn't going to tell you to "let go" or "just move on."

You already know you want to move on. You just don't know *how*.

So here's what we're going to do together:

We're going to find the piece that's been dragging you down – maybe it's guilt, maybe it's fear, maybe it's the voice in your head that keeps calling you names – and we're going to shine a light on it.

Not to shame it.

Not to rip it out like it doesn't belong.

But to understand it, shrink it down, and move it back where it belongs: off to the side. Not center stage.

Forgiving yourself doesn't mean pretending nothing happened. It means stopping the part of your brain that's been screaming at you nonstop. It means showing yourself the same basic kindness you'd give someone else.

It means saying:

"I'm still a good person. I just had a rough patch."

"I made a mistake, not a whole identity."

"I don't need to start over. I just need to *remember who I was before this got loud.*"

You're Allowed to Keep Going

This book is for the version of you that wants to feel okay again – even if you're scared you never will.

It's not here to judge you. It's not here to fix you.

It's here to walk beside you as you figure out how to take the weight off your own shoulders.

You don't need to be perfect.

You don't need to erase everything.

You just need to take the next step – with a little less fear, and a little more faith that you're worth the effort.

You are.

You really, really are.

Let's begin.

Chapter 1:
Everyone Screws Up

Let's get something out of the way right now:

You're going to mess up in life. You already have.
And guess what? So has everyone else.

Every single person you know has said something dumb, done something impulsive, hurt someone they cared about, or totally tanked a
situation they meant to handle better. And most of them probably
thought, in that moment:

"I'm the worst. What is wrong with me?"

We all get that sinking feeling in our gut at some point.
That "I just ruined everything" panic.
That "Why did I do that?" shame spiral.

If you've felt that?
Welcome. You're human. 🌐

The Myth of "Everyone Else" 🎭

It's easy to believe you're the only one who gets it wrong.

Other people walk around looking fine. They seem like they've got it together. They post smiley photos, crack jokes in class, act like they're totally unfazed by anything. It's easy to think,

"Maybe I'm just built differently. Maybe I'm the only one who keeps messing things up."

But here's what they don't show you:

- The guy who always looks chill? He cried in the bathroom last week after saying something he didn't mean.
- The girl who's crushing school? She's terrified she's going to lose control and disappoint everyone.
- The kid who seems like they don't care? They care more than anyone – but pretending not to helps them survive.

Most people are walking around wearing their best "I'm fine" mask. You just notice your mess more because you're stuck inside it.

Mistakes Come in All Shapes and Sizes 🔀

Maybe you:

- Lied to your parents
- Let a friend down
- Blew off school
- Cheated on a test
- Pushed someone away
- Ghosted somebody who didn't deserve it
- Screamed when you meant to stay calm
- Did something dumb that snowballed into something awful

Or maybe it's not even one big thing – it's a bunch of little choices that stacked up until you didn't recognize yourself anymore.

And maybe, right now, that's all you can see when you look in the mirror.

When a Mistake Becomes a Story 📖

Here's the dangerous part:
A mistake isn't just something that happens. It becomes a story in your head. And once that story takes root, it's hard to pull out.

You stop saying,
"I did something wrong."
and you start saying,
"I am wrong."

That's shame talking.
It takes something small and makes it sound like a final verdict on your entire character.

It tells you that because you messed up, you are a mess.
Because you failed, you are a failure.
Because you hurt someone, you are a bad person.

None of that is true. But it feels true when you're stuck inside it.

14

What If It Was Just... Life? 🏆

Sometimes what we call a screw-up is just being overwhelmed.

Maybe you didn't do the right thing because you didn't know what the right thing was. Or maybe you did know, but you didn't have the tools or the strength to follow through at the time. Maybe you were scared, tired, triggered, angry, exhausted – or just... lost.

That doesn't make you evil. That makes you in-progress.

You are not a finished product.
You are not a closed file.
You are someone still learning how to handle life – and that learning curve can be steep, especially when no one ever taught you how to manage emotions, make decisions, or bounce back from failure.

So yes. You probably screwed something up. Welcome to the club.
That doesn't disqualify you from becoming someone amazing.

You Are Not Alone 🤝

The voice in your head will try to tell you:

"Everyone else is fine. You're the broken one."

That voice is lying. Loudly.
But that lie is powerful, because it isolates you. It makes you pull away from people who care. It keeps you stuck in the idea that you're too far gone to be helped, or even seen.

Here's what's real:

You are not the only one who regrets something.
You are not the only one who wants a second chance.
You are not the only one trying to quietly fix your life while pretending nothing's wrong.

You are one of many.
And there's no shame in that.

What Matters Now 🎯

This book isn't going to erase what happened. That's not how life works.

What it can do is help you stop dragging that moment behind you like it defines everything.

You're not stuck in place. You're not doomed. You're not over.

You just hit a wall – and it hurt. But that wall? It's not the end. It's just something to climb over.

You're allowed to get back up.
You're allowed to heal.
You're allowed to be okay again – even if you're not sure how.

That's what we're going to figure out together.

📝 Mini Exercise ✏️

Make a short list of things you regret.
Big ones, small ones – whatever's weighing on you right now.

Now, beside each one, write the first step toward making peace with it.
Not fixing it. Not erasing it. Just something kind. Something honest. Something small.

Even if all you can write is, "I'm allowed to grow from this" – that's enough.

Chapter 2:
What You Did Isn't Who You Are

Let's say it straight:

Just because you did something wrong, doesn't mean you are something wrong.

You are not the worst moment of your life.
You are not the version of yourself that panicked, lashed out, shut down, or didn't show up.
You're not permanently stamped with that one failure, that one bad choice, or that one time you said or did something you wish you could erase.

You're not a villain in someone's story.
You're not a cautionary tale.
You're just someone who messed up – and is still learning.

And learning doesn't make you weak. It makes you growing. 🌱

The Shame Trap 🎭

Let's talk about shame.

Shame is the voice that says:

"You didn't just make a mistake – you ARE the mistake."

It's sneaky, too. It shows up in ways that feel familiar:

- "I can't believe I did that."
- "They'll never trust me again."
- "Maybe I deserve to feel like garbage."

But here's the problem with shame:
It doesn't help you grow.
It just paralyzes you.

Shame wants to keep you stuck in the past.
It wants you to wear the mistake like a name tag:

Hello, my name is: Regret

But that's not your name.

You are not a walking mistake.
You're a human who ran into something hard – and now you're here,
trying to move forward.

That's not failure. That's courage. 🧗

22

Guilt Is Different ⚖️

There's a difference between shame and guilt.

Guilt says, "I did something I'm not proud of."
It nudges you to apologize, repair, do better.

Shame says, "I am something to be ashamed of."
It tells you to disappear. To shut up. To stop trying.

Guilt can be helpful.
Shame is poison.

Here's the trick: Learn to sit with guilt long enough to learn from it – but not so long that it turns into shame.

Guilt says, "That wasn't like me."
Shame says, "That's all I am."
You get to decide which voice wins. 🗣️

You're Bigger Than the Worst Thing You've Done 🏔️

Let's zoom out for a second.

Think about your entire life – not just today, not just last week. All of it. Every memory, every kind thing you've done, every effort, every time you helped someone or made someone laugh or quietly tried to do the right thing even when no one noticed.

Now compare that to the one thing you did that keeps haunting you.

Does that one moment erase everything else?

No.
But shame wants you to think it does.

It wants to zoom in so close on the screw-up that everything else fades away.
It wants you to believe that people are only allowed to be one thing: good or bad, kind or cruel, worthy or not.

But people aren't that simple.
You aren't that simple.

You're a mix of good and bad, strong and scared, healing and hurting. You're learning. That doesn't make you less – it makes you real. ❋

Let Yourself Be Seen 👀

You might be afraid that if people really knew you – the real you – they'd walk away. But what if the opposite is true?

What if being honest about your struggle actually makes you more human?

What if someone else is waiting to hear exactly what you're too scared to say?

When you start believing that what you did isn't the same as who you are, something shifts.

You start walking with your head up again.
You start speaking like your voice matters.
You start realizing that one mistake doesn't cancel your whole story.

You start living again. 🌈

📝 Mini Exercise 🖊️

Write a short letter from your future self to the version of you who made the mistake.

Not a letter of punishment.
A letter of kindness.

Let it say:

- "You didn't know better yet."
- "You were hurting."
- "I forgive you."

Write like you'd talk to your best friend. Because that's what you need right now – a friend inside yourself.

Chapter 3:
The Voice in Your Head is a Jerk

You know the one.

That voice that shows up right after you mess up – or even just think about messing up – and goes straight for the kill:

"You're such an idiot."
"Of course you blew it."
"You always do this."
"Why would anyone want to deal with you?"

It's that voice that makes you cringe at night when you're trying to fall asleep. The one that replays awkward moments, repeats every failure in high-definition, and mutters horrible things about you that you'd never say to someone else.

So let's be clear about something:

That voice is not the truth.
It's not your "real self."
And it's definitely not helping.

It's just a scared, loud, pushy narrator with no volume control and way too much free time. 🎙️

Where That Voice Comes From

Nobody's born hating themselves.

That mean voice in your head? It got built.
Piece by piece, over time. From things you heard. From the way you were treated. From pressure, expectations, pain, or stuff you didn't even realize was getting stored in the back of your brain like bad files.

Sometimes it sounds like your parents. Or your teachers. Or a bully. Sometimes it sounds like you, but harsher and meaner.

It builds itself from things people say when they're angry, or things you believed because no one told you otherwise.

Eventually, it starts to feel familiar. Like background noise.

But just because it's familiar doesn't mean it's right.

Your Brain Is Not Always on Your Side 🧠

Here's the wild part: Your brain is trying to protect you.

Weird, right?

The inner jerk voice is basically your brain saying,

"If I point out the mistake first, you'll be safe. If I'm hard on you, maybe you won't mess up again. If I call you worthless, at least no one else can beat me to it."

It's messed up. But it makes sense, in a twisted kind of way.

Your brain thinks it's helping you stay safe by being mean.
Like if it criticizes you first, no one else can hurt you.
But instead of keeping you safe, it just keeps you small.

You Don't Have to Believe It 🚫 💬

You can't always stop the voice from showing up.
But you can stop believing it.

You can learn to treat it like background noise. Static. Unreliable narration.

You can learn to talk back.

When it says, "You always screw up," you say:
"Actually, I've gotten through a lot. And I'm still here."

When it says, "No one's ever going to forgive you," you say:
"People surprise me. And I'm learning to forgive myself."

When it says, "You're just too much," you say:
"I'm not too much. I'm just more than that voice can handle."

You don't have to be louder than the voice.
You just have to stop letting it run the whole show. 🔲

Roast That Voice 🐵

One of the fastest ways to deflate a shame voice is to make fun of it.

No really – give it a name.

Not a cool one. Not a serious one. A stupid one. Something ridiculous, like:

- Blurticus the Loudmouth
- Captain Self-Doubt
- Negative Nancy 9000
- Doomweasel
- Kevin. Just... Kevin. (Unless that's YOUR name – then choose a different one).

Next time it pipes up with:
"You'll never get past this,"
you can say:
"Thanks for your input, Kevin. Kindly shut up."

Sometimes you don't need deep healing. You just need to interrupt the broadcast and laugh a little. 😄

Talk to Yourself Like Someone You Like 🖤

Imagine your best friend came to you and said:
"I made a mistake. I feel awful. I think I might be a bad person."

Would you scream at them?
Would you tell them they're garbage?
Would you say they don't deserve a second chance?

No. You'd probably say:
"You're not a bad person. You're just having a hard time. Let's figure it out."

So why not say that to yourself?

You live inside your own head. Might as well make it a safer place to be. 🏠

📝 Mini Exercise ✏️

Give your inner critic a name. (The dumber, the better.)
Write down three things it always says to you.
Now – write a response to each one. Make it kind. Make it honest.
Or just tell Kevin to take a nap. 🔍

Chapter 4:
You Don't Need to Be Perfect to Make Things Right

Okay, let's talk about fixing it.

You messed up.
You hurt someone.
You made a choice that didn't go how you thought.
Or maybe you didn't do something you should have done.

Now it's sitting on your chest like a giant emotional laundry pile, and every time you try to move on, it crunches underfoot and says,

"You can't leave this here."

Cool. Let's talk about how to clean it up.

But first – you don't need to be perfect to make things right.
You just need to be honest.

You Don't Owe the World a Performance 🎭

You don't have to cry a certain amount.

You don't have to write a 12-page apology letter or memorize a TED Talk.

You don't have to over-apologize forever, then disappear into a hole of guilt until someone lets you out.

You don't have to suffer to be sorry.

All you need is to:

- Own what happened
- Acknowledge how it affected someone else
- Say what you're doing to grow from it

That's it.

That's an apology.

Anything beyond that is guilt trying to audition for an Oscar. 🏆

Real Apologies vs. Guilt Theater

Here's what a real apology sounds like:

"I know I hurt you. I wasn't thinking clearly, and I wish I had handled it differently. I understand why you're upset, and I'm working on it. I don't expect anything – I just wanted to say I'm sorry."

Here's what guilt theater sounds like:

"I'm the worst. I ruin everything. You must hate me. I don't deserve forgiveness. Please forgive me even though I'm trash."

See the difference?

One centers the person you hurt.
The other centers your own pain.

Apologizing isn't about making someone feel bad for being hurt.
It's about recognizing the impact you had – and giving them space to feel it.

When They Don't Forgive You

Yeah, this part sucks. Sometimes, you do the work. You say the right thing. You really mean it. And the other person still says:

"Nope. I'm done."

Or worse, they ignore you completely.

That doesn't mean your apology was useless.
That doesn't mean you're a monster.
That means they get to choose their healing too – and sometimes that means letting go.

You don't get to control how someone responds.
You just get to control your own integrity.

If you did the right thing with an open heart, that matters – even if they never say a word back. 💜

Sometimes You're the One Who Was Hurt 💜

Let's not skip this part:
Sometimes the mistake wasn't yours.
Sometimes someone else hurt you – and you've been carrying the blame.

Maybe they never apologized.
Maybe they made you feel like it was your fault.
Maybe you've been treating yourself like the villain in someone else's story.

You are allowed to forgive yourself for surviving someone else's bad behavior.

You are allowed to say:
"That wasn't on me. And I don't have to carry it anymore."

This chapter isn't just about apologizing to others.
It's also about making peace with yourself. 🕊️

Fixing Doesn't Mean Forgetting 🪶

You're not trying to erase what happened. You're trying to learn from it.

Owning your mistake doesn't mean pretending it didn't hurt.
It means saying:
"I get it now. And I'm doing better on purpose."

That's real growth. That's character.
Not some flawless reputation – but quiet, steady responsibility.

You Can Start Small

Not ready for a big conversation yet? That's okay.

Try this:

- Write a letter you don't send yet
- Say sorry in your own head first
- Do one tiny thing to show change (even if no one notices)

You're building trust again – maybe with someone else, maybe with yourself.

It doesn't have to be loud. It just has to be true.

📝 Mini Exercise ✍️

Write two short letters.

1. One is an apology.
   It can be for something recent or something old. Be honest, not dramatic.

2. The other is a release.
   Let go of something someone else did to you. You don't need to excuse it – you're just saying you're done holding it like it's your job to fix.

You don't have to show these to anyone.

Sometimes healing starts in private. 🔍

Chapter 5:
It's Never Too Late to Stop the Spiral

So, you messed up. Maybe more than once.

Maybe it wasn't just a single bad day, but a string of them.

Maybe it feels like things got off track a while ago and now you're too far gone to fix it.

That's the lie. That right there – is the lie that keeps people stuck.

"I already blew it. What's the point?"
"I'm already failing. Might as well just give up."
"They already think I'm a problem, so whatever."

That's not truth. That's shame trying to hand you a shovel.

Spiraling Doesn't Mean You Can't Stop

Let's say you skipped one assignment. Okay, that's not great. But now you're panicking, and instead of turning that one thing in late, you avoid the whole class. Now you've missed three more. You stop showing up altogether. You convince yourself it's pointless.

That's a spiral.
Not a plan.

One bad choice doesn't mean you have to follow it with ten more. And you definitely don't have to stay stuck just because you've been stuck.

You're Allowed to Change Course Midway 🔄

We have this weird idea in our heads that once we start a pattern, we have to finish it.

Like:

- "I already blew off this semester, so I might as well flunk the year."
- "I already lost their trust, so why even bother being honest now?"
- "I already embarrassed myself, so I'll just keep being the screw-up."

That's not logic. That's emotional damage control.
You're trying to get ahead of the pain by rejecting yourself before anyone else can.

But here's the truth:
You can stop at any point.
You can shift course mid-slide.
You don't need permission.
You just need the moment you choose to try.

What "Recovery" Really Looks Like 🌱

Getting your life back on track doesn't mean pretending none of it happened. It means making a turn – even if it's small, even if it's awkward, even if you still have stuff to clean up.

Recovery might look like:

- Emailing the teacher even though you're embarrassed
- Telling a friend, "I wasn't okay for a while. I want to try now."
- Cleaning your room and doing laundry after weeks of giving up 🧺
- Admitting that you weren't "fine" and don't want to keep pretending

None of those things erase the past.

They just start building a future that isn't ruled by it. 🧱

Don't Throw the Whole Thing Out

If your phone glitches, you restart it.
You don't throw it in the ocean.

But we treat ourselves like if one thing goes wrong, the whole system is broken. And that's just not how it works.

- Failing a class isn't the end of your future.
- Having a bad relationship doesn't mean you're incapable of love.
- Losing control doesn't mean you'll never get it back.

You don't have to trash the whole story.

You just have to flip the page.

You're Still Worth the Effort ◈

Even if you've messed up a bunch.
Even if you've burned bridges.
Even if people have started expecting the worst from you.

You are still worth saving.

You are still worth the work.

And most of all? You're still capable of a life you feel good about – even if it starts with a single, shaky step back toward center. 👣

📝 Mini Exercise ✏️

Pick one thing you've given up on.
Now write down one small action that could shift the direction – even slightly.

Examples:

- Missed every homework assignment? Turn in one.
- Ghosted a friend? Text them a meme.
- Avoiding everything? Make your bed. One corner counts.

This isn't about fixing it all at once.

It's about choosing not to spiral today. 🔍

Chapter 6:
You Can't Undo It – So What Now?

Let's be honest.
There are things you can't take back.

You can apologize.
You can grow.
You can make things right – or at least try.

But you can't go back in time and un-say it, un-do it, un-feel it.

Sometimes that's the hardest part.
Not the mistake itself – but the part where you have to live with it.

And maybe you're thinking:
"I don't know if I can. I don't know how to be okay knowing I did that."

But here's the truth: you don't need to erase the past to build a better future.

You just need to stop letting the past be the only thing driving the car.
🚗

Living <u>With</u> the Memory vs. Living <u>In</u> It

There's a difference between remembering and replaying.

Remembering means saying:
"Yeah, that happened. I don't like it. But I've learned from it."

Replaying means saying:
"Let me relive this over and over again until I feel worse than I did when it actually happened."

You are not required to put yourself through a guilt loop to prove you care.

Caring means doing better.

Not punishing yourself forever.

The Weight Gets Lighter 🎒

At first, it feels like you're carrying a backpack full of bricks.

You think about it constantly. You second-guess yourself. You hear echoes of what you did, and every time you feel a little bit smaller.

But over time – if you let yourself heal – the backpack gets lighter.

The memory doesn't disappear, but it stops being so sharp.
It becomes part of your story, but not the title.

You stop waking up feeling like a criminal.
You start realizing you're still a person – just one who's been through something, and come out stronger. 💪

You Don't Have to Be Haunted 👻

Yes, you hurt someone. Yes, you disappointed yourself.
Yes, maybe things would be different if you had handled it another way.

But dragging that around like a ghost doesn't undo it.
It just hurts you twice.

You are allowed to say:
"I hate what happened. I own it. But I don't want it to define me."

You don't have to be haunted by your past.
You can honor it, learn from it, and walk forward anyway. 🚶

Growth Doesn't Erase the Past – It Changes the Future 🪴 📖

Sometimes we get stuck trying to make up for what we did by being perfect now.

- You try to be the best friend ever because you were a bad one once.
- You try to be flawless in class because you failed last semester.
- You try to be quiet and "good" because once, you lost control.

But perfection isn't the answer.
You don't need to live the rest of your life as a punishment or a cover-up.

You just need to live it differently – with more care, more clarity, and more courage.

That's growth.

You're Not That Person Anymore 🔑

Even if it was yesterday.
Even if it was an hour ago.
The moment you realized you want to do better – you became some-
one else.

Not perfect. Not finished. Just different.
More aware. More intentional. More honest.

You don't have to carry who you were.
You just have to walk with who you are becoming. 🌸

📝 Mini Exercise ✍️

Write this sentence:

"I can't undo _____, but I can _____."

Fill in the blanks honestly.

Examples:

- I can't undo failing last semester, but I can show up for this one.
- I can't undo the lie I told, but I can be honest moving forward.
- I can't undo hurting them, but I can be better to the people I love now.
- I can't undo disappearing when it mattered, but I can stay now.

This isn't about fixing the past.

It's about freeing your future. 🚀

Chapter 7:
When You Keep Messing Up Anyway

So you decided to turn things around.

You apologized. You journaled. You even made a list of next steps and taped it to your wall.

And then... you messed up again.

You snapped. You skipped. You ghosted. You spiraled.
You did the very thing you promised yourself you wouldn't do.

And now what?
Back to square one?

Nope. Not even close.

Growth Is Messy 🖊

Real talk: self-improvement doesn't happen in a straight line.

You don't just say "I want to be better" and magically become a shiny, problem-free version of yourself. If only.

Growth looks like:

- Three good days. One disaster. Then another try.
- Two steps forward. One step back. Repeat.
- Doing better, then falling on your face, then getting back up anyway.

That doesn't mean you're failing.
That means you're learning.

Even people with the best intentions backslide. Even people with all the right tools fall into old patterns. That doesn't make you weak – it makes you human.

Why You Might Still Be Struggling 🧠 💾

Let's say you're trying to stop a behavior – maybe it's avoiding respon-
sibilities, getting defensive, or blowing things off when they get hard.

You want to stop. You mean it.

So why does it keep happening?

Because patterns don't break just because you want them to.
They break when you figure out what's triggering them.

Your brain is still running the same old program.

You've just started questioning it.

What's Behind the Mess? 🕵️

Most of the time, when we mess up repeatedly, it's not about laziness or weakness.

It's about:

- Fear
- Anxiety
- Exhaustion
- Pressure
- Trying to protect yourself, even if it doesn't make sense

You might lash out to push people away before they leave you.
You might give up before you fail so you can say, "Whatever, I didn't care anyway."

You might check out emotionally because feeling stuff is overwhelming.

None of that makes you broken.
It just means your coping strategies are outdated – and they're no longer helping.

The Goal Isn't Perfection – It's Awareness 🎯

When you mess up again, try asking:

- "What was I feeling right before this happened?"
- "What was I trying to avoid or protect myself from?"
- "What would I do differently if I could rewind 10 minutes?"

Even just asking these questions means you're growing.

That little pause? That little moment of reflection?
That's the difference between spiraling and rerouting. 🎇

You Don't Lose All Progress Because You Had a Bad Moment 📖

You're not at zero. You're not disqualified. You didn't ruin everything.

One mess-up doesn't delete all your effort.
It's not a factory reset.
It's just... a stumble.

You get to keep going from where you are – knowledge, strength, healing, all still intact.

The version of you that wants to be better is still here.
That part didn't disappear. It just got quiet for a second.

Let's turn the volume back up. 🔊

📝 Mini Exercise ✍

Think about a moment when you "messed up again."

Now answer these three questions honestly:

1. What was going on before the mistake?

2. What need were you trying to meet (even in a messed-up way)?

3. What's one small change that might help next time?

You don't have to get it perfect.
You just have to get curious. 🔍

Chapter 8:
Small Wins Still Count

Let's be honest.
Most progress doesn't feel like a movie montage.

There's no dramatic music.
No spotlight.
No teacher clapping as you turn your life around in one epic gesture.

Most real progress looks more like:

- Getting out of bed when you didn't want to
- Replying to a message instead of ghosting
- Putting your phone down and doing five minutes of something hard
- Not saying that one thing you really wanted to say in the heat of the moment

It's not flashy.
It's not dramatic.

But it counts. ✅

You're Building Something – Even If You Can't See It Yet 🧱

Think of every small win like a brick.
Not much on its own. But keep stacking them, and one day you've got something solid.

The problem is, most people throw away the first 20 bricks because the building doesn't look like anything yet.

They say:
"I only went to class once this week – big deal."
"I said one nice thing today. So what?"
"I only made it halfway through my to-do list."

But you know what? That's still a win.

Half the battle is showing up.

The other half is not quitting just because it's not perfect yet.

How to Spot a Win 🏅

If you're waiting for someone else to hand you a trophy for doing better, you're going to be waiting a long time.

So give yourself credit.

A win is anything that:
- Pushes you slightly out of your comfort zone
- Moves you one inch closer to the version of you you want to be
- Interrupts a negative pattern, even once

Even thinking differently about something you usually avoid?

That's a win. That's your brain rewiring. ⚡

You Are Allowed to Be Proud of Small Things

Say this out loud (or whisper it if someone's nearby):

"I'm allowed to feel good about something even if it's small."

Because guess what? Shame loves to convince you that small wins don't matter.

Shame wants you to believe:
"If it's not life-changing, it's worthless."

But growth doesn't show up all at once.
It shows up in quiet moments where you made a better choice, even if no one saw it.

You saw it. That's enough.

Consistency Beats Intensity ⊜

Anyone can be great for a day.
Anyone can make a huge change in a burst of energy.

But what actually transforms your life?

Small, repeated effort.
The kind that feels boring. The kind that's easy to overlook.
The kind that doesn't make a good TikTok but does make a better life.

You don't need to go big.
You just need to keep going.

You're Doing Better Than You Think 👀

Seriously. You are.

If you've read this far in this book?
If you've reflected on even one thing that hurt and how to do better?

You're ahead of the curve.

You don't have to wait until you're fixed to celebrate yourself.

You get to be proud on the way there. 🎉

📝 Mini Exercise ✍️

Make a **"win list"** from the last 7 days.

No win is too small. Include anything that:

- Helped you keep going
- Interrupted a bad habit
- Showed effort, even if it didn't work out perfectly

Then circle your favorite one. That's your proof that you're not stuck. You're moving. 🔍

Chapter 9:
You Get to Like Yourself Again

There's something no one tells you after you've messed up:

You're allowed to like yourself again.

Not later. Not once you've "proven" yourself.
Not after you've done some dramatic apology tour or earned back 100% trust from the entire universe.

Now.
Even while you're still healing.
Even while you're still figuring it out.

You get to look in the mirror and say:
"Hey. I'm doing okay."

And if you can't quite say that yet?

We'll work on it. 🔍

Liking Yourself Isn't Narcissistic 🚫 🤍

Let's get something straight: liking yourself is not bragging.
It's not ego. It's not arrogance. It's not "thinking you're better than everyone."

It's literally just deciding not to treat yourself like garbage anymore.

It's being on your own side.

It's saying:

- "I care about how I treat people, and I include myself in that."
- "I want to get better, and I think I deserve that chance."
- "I don't want to live in self-loathing forever."

That's not pride. That's survival. 🌱

You Don't Have to Wait for Full Redemption 🏺

There's this unspoken rule people carry around:
"I'll like myself when I've fixed everything."

That's like saying:
"I'll drink water once I'm no longer thirsty."

You need self-respect to fuel the healing process.
You need self-compassion to have the energy to keep trying.
You can't shame yourself into being whole.

You can't hate yourself into becoming someone you love. 🦅

Find the Small Things Worth Liking 🧱 ✨

Maybe you're not ready to say, "I love myself." Totally fair.

Let's aim for:

- "I like that I keep trying."
- "I like that I'm honest, even when it's awkward."
- "I like that I care."
- "I like that I made my bed today. That was weirdly satisfying."
- "I like that I didn't completely give up, even when it would've been easier."

That's enough.

Those small things?
Those are the **bricks** 🧱 we talked about.
That's how you build something real – something strong – without ever needing a spotlight.

Most people will never get a chance to do something "heroic."
But every one of us gets the chance, every day, to do something kind, something honest, or something better than we would have done last year.

That's how you win your way back to yourself. 🏆

Liking Yourself Doesn't Mean Ignoring the Past 📖

You don't have to pretend nothing happened.

You don't have to gloss over the hurt.

You just have to say:

"Even with all of that, I'm still someone worth rooting for."

That's not denial. That's grace. ✦

And grace is what helps people move forward with dignity.

People Will Follow Your Lead 👣

You want people to stop judging you by your worst moment?
Start showing them how you treat yourself now.

Not by bragging. Not by pretending.
But by quietly living like you matter.

You'd be surprised how quickly others pick up on it.
Confidence isn't about volume. It's about alignment.

When you carry yourself like someone you respect, the world adjusts.
🌍

📝 Mini Exercise 🖊️

Write down **five things you like about yourself.**
Not things you wish were true – things that already are.

If you get stuck, try:

- "I like the way I..."
- "I like that I've been willing to..."
- "I like that I keep..."
- "I like that I care about..."

Circle one and make it your reminder for the week.
Tape it up. Text it to yourself. Make it your lock screen. Whatever works.

You don't have to wait for permission to feel okay again.

You're the one who gets to give that. 💎

Chapter 10:
You're Already on Your Way

You made it to the end of the book.
And guess what?

That means you're not stuck.
You're not frozen in guilt.
You're not too far gone.

You're already moving.

Even if it doesn't feel like it.
Even if you're still unsure.
Even if you still have rough days, bad patterns, and stuff you wish you could redo.

You're still here.
You're still reading.
You're still reaching for something better.

That counts.

You Don't Need to Start Over – Just Start From Here 📖

Forget the idea that you need a clean slate.
Forget the idea that you need to "get back to who you used to be."

You're not going back. You're going forward.

You've learned things now. You've faced hard truths. You've felt pain and regret and growth and maybe even a little hope.

That doesn't make you broken.

That makes you ready. 🔹

Let Go of the Reset Button 🔄

The world sells this idea of "fresh starts" like they're magical:
New year, new you. New semester. New job. New vibe.

But real healing? It doesn't come from a reset button.
It comes from continuing – even when it's awkward. Even when it's messy. Even when it's not very Instagram-worthy.

It comes from saying:
"This is where I am. And this is where I'm headed."

You're not rebooting. You're rebuilding. 🧱

Look at How Far You've Already Come 👣

Seriously. Take a second.

- You named something you regret
- You looked at the part of you that hurt someone – or hurt yourself
- You admitted you want to do better
- You read a whole book about forgiving yourself

That's not nothing.

That's the beginning of something really good. ✨

You Still Get to Write the Rest of the Story 📝 📖

You are not a failure.
You're a person in progress.

And the story isn't over.

Every day you wake up, you get another line. Another paragraph. Another chance to turn the page and add something new.

You're not rewriting the past.
You're adding context to it.
You're showing what came next.

So when people look back on that low point someday, they won't say:
"That's where it ended."

They'll say:
"That's where everything started to change."

📝 Mini Exercise: The Permission Slip ✍️

Write this sentence and sign it:

**"I don't have to be perfect. I just have to keep trying.
I forgive myself for what I didn't know then.
I trust myself to do better now.
I am worth the effort."**

Sign your name underneath.
Say it out loud if you're feeling brave.

You don't need anyone else's approval to move forward.

This is yours to claim. 🩶

Final Reminder

You are not a bad person.

You are not broken beyond repair.

You are not the worst thing you've ever done.

You are capable. You are learning. You are growing.

And you are already on your way.

Conclusion:
You're Still Becoming

If you're still here – if you made it through all the pages, all the reflection, all the hard thoughts and honest exercises – then I want you to hear this one more time:

You are not a failure.

You are not too far gone.

You are not beyond repair.

You are **becoming.**

That doesn't always feel like growth. Sometimes it feels like confusion. Or sadness. Or exhaustion. Or standing still when everyone else seems to be sprinting ahead.

But becoming isn't always loud.
Sometimes it's quiet.
Sometimes it's the decision to try again when no one's watching.
Sometimes it's just taking a breath and choosing not to quit.

You're the One Who Gets to Decide 🔑

No one else gets to decide what you're allowed to move on from.
No one else gets to measure your worth.
No one else knows the full story of what you've been carrying 👜 .

Only you.

And you don't owe anyone some dramatic, perfect comeback story.

You just owe yourself the chance to keep going.

Let This Be a Beginning

This book was never meant to fix you.
Because you weren't broken.

It was just here to walk beside you for a little while, remind you of your worth , and hand you a few tools to help you stand a little taller.

The rest? That's yours.

You're allowed to keep stumbling.
You're allowed to mess up again.

But now – you've got a map. You've got a voice in your head that's a little kinder.

You've got evidence that you can move forward, even with the past behind you.

So go live it. Go write the next chapter.

You're still you.
You're still becoming.

And you are still allowed to like who you are becoming – even as you grow.

A Note to Adults

This book wasn't written to diagnose or discipline.

It was written to sit beside a young person when they feel alone in their own regret.

Teens carry a lot – more than we sometimes realize. And when they mess up, their first instinct is often to spiral inward. To assume they're ruined. To believe they're defined by that one moment, or that one version of themselves.

This book speaks to the quiet in-between. It helps them separate who they *are* from what they *did*, and gives them the space to move forward with dignity.

If you're a parent, teacher, counselor, or trusted adult:

Thank you for offering this book to a young person who needed it.

Please know that your presence, patience, and willingness to listen without judgment will do more than any chapter ever could.

You don't have to have all the answers.

Just being someone who believes they can do better is already enough.

About This Book

This book is part of the *Can't I Just...* series, written to help teens handle real-life challenges with confidence, clarity, and compassion. *Can't I Just Start Over?* was created for anyone who's struggling with regret, shame, or the feeling that they're "not a good person" because of something they said or did. It offers practical tools and supportive guidance for teens who want to make amends, learn from their mistakes, and move forward without losing themselves in guilt.

About the Author

Jennifer Larsen is the founder of Wayfinder Press and the Wayfinder Foundation. With a background in education, psychology, and leadership, she writes books designed to help kids, teens, and adults handle real life with clarity, confidence, and compassion. Her work focuses on emotional growth, life skills, and decision-making – always with a warm, honest tone that meets readers where they are.

Thank You

If this book helped you, we'd love to hear from you! Your reviews and shares help us reach more teens who need a little extra support.

Explore the Full Series

The *Can't I Just...* series helps kids and teens navigate real-life challenges with honesty, humor, and practical tools. Each book stands alone, but together they offer a well-rounded foundation for emotional growth, career exploration, and everyday life skills.

Other titles include:

- *Can't I Just Stay in My Room?* – A career guide for teens who don't know what they want to be yet
- *Can't I Just Skip College?* – Real alternatives to the four-year path
- *Can't I Just Help My Kid Pick a Path?* – A guide for parents helping kids with career questions
- *Can't I Just Be Like Everyone Else?* – A soft skills survival guide for teens
- *Can't I Just Hit Reset?* – Self-forgiveness and emotional recovery for kids

To see the full list or download companion materials as they become available, visit **CantIJust.com**

About Wayfinder Foundation Inc.

This book is part of a nonprofit mission.

Wayfinder Foundation Inc. provides educational tools, resources, and programming to help youth and adults explore careers, build life skills, and improve emotional resilience. We believe everyone deserves support, no matter their path.

To learn more or support our mission, visit:

WayfinderFoundationInc.org